WEST END ORGANIX

Ageless Beauty, Organic Health

Look and feel younger and healthier with our natural remedies products!

www.WestEndOrganix.com

Discount: 10% off of your order - Code *WEO2021*

Pump it up Magazine

TABLE OF CONTENTS

EDITORIAL — Page 5

CARTER KAYA — 6
From War-Torn Congo to the Parisian Music Scene: The Journey of Carter Kaya, the Prodigiously Talented Artis, Music Executive and Business Man

BLACK HISTORY MONTH — 10
- Was The Green Book a Guide to Freedom or a Constraint on Black Travel?
- The Evolution of Soul Food:
- Celebrating the Contributions of Black Artists, Writers, and Performers

HAPPY VALENTINE'S DAY
- How and Where to find your soulmate

FITNESS
- Couple's Workouts

DISCOVER YOUR TRUE SELF — 21
Being single on Valentine's Day. Know Thyself

MOVIES — 27
Classic Love Stories

TOP TIPS
Indie Artists How To Book Your Next Gigs

HUMANITARIAN AWARENESS
Rebuilding Hope: Supporting the Victims of the Syria and Turkey Earthquake

Pump it up MAGAZINE ®

PUMP IT UP MAGAZINE
LINKS

WEBSITE
www.pumpitupmagazine.com

FACEBOOK
www.facebook.com/pumpitupmagazine

TWITTER
www.twitter.com/pumpitupmag

SOUNDCLOUD
www.soundcloud.com/pumpitupmagazine

INSTAGRAM
pumpitupmagazine

PINTEREST
www.pinterest.com/pumpitupmagazine

PUMP IT UP MAGAZINE
30721 Russell Ranch Road
Suite 140
Westlake Village,
California 91362
United States

 (818)514 – 0038(Ext:102)
 info@pumpitupmagazine.com

EDITORIAL

Greeting Readers!

In this month's issue of Pump It Up Magazine, we are proud to celebrate not only the incredible journey of Carter Kaya, the visionary leader of the French musical empire Delit Music France, but also the contributions of black artists, writers, and performers in honor of Black History Month.

From his humble beginnings in war-torn Congo to his rise as a highly-respected and sought-after music executive, Carter's journey is a testament to the power of perseverance, talent, and determination. We delve into his story, exploring how he navigated the challenges and obstacles he faced along the way, and discover what sets Delit Music France apart from other musical empires.

Alongside Carter's story, this issue of Pump It Up Magazine also offers a range of diverse and thought-provoking articles. For those looking to improve their fitness and relationships, we explore the benefits of couple's workouts. And for those navigating the ups and downs of being single on Valentine's Day, we delve into the journey of self-discovery and the importance of knowing oneself.

In addition, we shine a spotlight on classic love stories in movies and celebrate the season of love by exploring the history and evolution of soul food, a rich culinary tradition with roots in African American culture.
We also bring awareness to important humanitarian issues, such as supporting the victims of the recent Syria-Turkey earthquake.

So whether you're a music lover, fitness enthusiast, or simply someone looking to broaden your horizons, this issue of Pump It Up Magazine
has something for everyone.

As we celebrate Black History Month and Valentine's Day, we hope to inspire, educate, and entertain our readers, and to continue to promote diversity, inclusiveness, and awareness.

Anissa Sutton

CONTRIBUTORS

FOUNDER
Anissa Sutton

EDITOR
Michael B. Sutton

FASHION
Tiffani Sutton

MARKETING
Grace Rose

PARTNERS

Editions L.A.
www.editions-la.com

The Sound Of L.A.
www.thesoundofla.com

Info Music
www.infomusic.fr

L.A. Unlimited
www.launlimitedinc.com

CARTER KAYA

— Artist & Businesss Man —

FROM WAR-TORN CONGO TO THE PARISIAN MUSIC SCENE: A TRIUMPHANT STORY.

Meet Carter, a rising star hailing from the Congo who has not only overcome tremendous odds to become the talented artist he is today, but also a successful music executive. Born and raised in several cities in Congo Brazzaville during a time of violence and conflict, Carter was witness to the devastating effects of war. Despite these traumatic experiences, music provided him with solace and a source of inspiration to pursue his dream of becoming an artist.

Growing up in a broken family with divorced parents, Carter was drawn to sports and excelled at football and acrobatics. Despite having to move frequently with his father for work, Carter never lost his love for music, discovering it for the first time through the song "Caroline" by MC Solaar on RFI radio. This pivotal moment sparked a passion within him, leading him to rewrite song lyrics and perform in singing contests in his neighborhood.

At just 15 years old, Carter took on a job as a carpenter to support his passion for music, using his earnings to purchase better quality reading materials. On weekends, he hosted musical evenings in front of his house, quickly becoming known as a talented DJ.

Despite the hardships brought on by the war, Carter's determination and perseverance have paid off. He was sent to Italy at 15 years old to continue his studies and pursue his dream of becoming an artist, and today he is a globally recognized talent with a thriving music career.

But Carter's achievements don't stop there. He is also a successful music executive who has developed his own record label, DMG Records, and released compilations with many Parisian artists. He also owns a promotion company, DELIT MUSIC (www.delitmusic.fr), and INFO MUSIC MAG (www.infomusicmag.fr), helping to support and showcase the talent of other artists.

Carter's life story is a testament to the power of hope and the unwavering spirit of the human soul. He continues to inspire young people everywhere, spreading his music and message of hope to future generations while also providing opportunities for other artists to succeed through his businesses

Carter's Journey from

CONGO ITALY FRANCE

Discovering the Beauty of Music Through Adversity

"That time in Congo was very anxiety-inducing for me. Sometimes, at checkpoints, I had to wait for two hours to be checked and during that time, I saw corpses and people killed right in front of me because they belonged to another tribe. Once, I was checked and I had forgotten my papers. I could have been killed on the spot if a man who knew me had not intervened to tell the militants that "I know this kid, he's the child of the colonel's friend." Hearing this, I saw fear in the militants' eyes..."

"As a child at that time, I did not realize death until it happened to me. I also experienced what I consider to be a special experience. We were at a checkpoint when we realized that people were shooting at us from a mountain. The checkpoint militants asked us to run into a forest to avoid being killed. Dressed in our school uniforms, we ran and detoured through the forest. There were about twenty of us and I arrived at school with my uniform all dirty. I explained to my history teacher what had happened to me. He looked at me and said "If you didn't wash your uniform yesterday, it's not useful to stay in my class today." He sent me to the principal who punished me by asking me to clean the school yard."

Coming from a broken family and having divorced parents, he grew up in the world of sports and playing football and doing acrobatics. However, due to his father who had to move often for his job, Carter often had to move around like a vagabond.

His first encounter with music took place during the war in the country, while he was listening to RFI radio. He was immediately captivated by the rhythms of MC Solaar's song "Caroline" and this inspired him to become an artist in turn.

"My first musical experience took place during the war in the country, in my room. I was listening to RFI Radio and heard the song "Caroline" by rapper MC Solaar and suddenly, I was carried away by the rhythms of his song that were:
"Claude MC takes the microphone, like a love story raggamuffin To talk to you about a friend we call Caroline She was my lady, she was my came She was my vitamin She was my drug, my dope, my coke, my crack My amphetamine, Caroline)."

He began re-writing the lyrics of MC Solaar's songs he heard on the radio and memorizing them by heart, then he participated in singing contests in his neighborhood. Over the years, he began to take an interest in other genres of music, such as Michael Jackson, Karyn White, Stevie Wonder and Claude François.

CARTER KAYA
THE MUSIC EXECUTIVE

CONGO ITALY FRANCE

AND BUSINESS MAN

ITALY:

Carter Kaya was sent to Italy by his parents at the age of 15, but instead of viewing this as a source of loneliness, Carter considers this a new life experience. He is naturally curious and likes to go after what he wants, which helped him avoid loneliness.

As a musician, Carter quickly found his place in Italy. He received project proposals and participated in Italian hip-hop group shows, such as Articolo 31. He was also sought after to perform at night clubs in Rome, Milan, Padua, Vicenza, Bassano and Padua.

These youthful experiences in Italy had a significant impact on Carter's personality and musical style. He found that there were few black singers in Italian music and this gave him the opportunity to show Italians another side of blacks living in Italy, both musically and fashion-wise

*"My arrival in Italy allowed me to notice that here were few black singers in music.
So, for me, it was easy to show the Italians another facet of the blacks living in Italy, either in the musical aspect or in the fashion aspect."*

FRANCE:

Carter then moved to Paris to further his music career. Inspired by the shortage of black singers in Italy, Carter wanted to show another side of the life of Blacks in Italy in terms of music and fashion. Encouragement from his business manager and a seasoned fellow countryman encouraged him to pursue his musical dreams and set greater goals.

Upon arriving in Paris, Carter created a home studio with equipment brought from Italy and a musical association called "DMG Records", which allowed him to produce his first work with his first wife, singer Lise. He also participated in several music shows to make himself known in the Parisian music scene.

Through encounters with artists, producers, bookers, and production labels, Carter evolved his musical style. He also had the opportunity to collaborate with artists such as Aneessa, Dorsey Sick Joker, Krime Mind, Tyron, B-La, Kaya, Tracy, Alison, Express Omega, and Lise while producing his Hip Hop/RnB compilation "The 2K Studio".

"This move from Italy to Paris allowed me to discover new musical influences, meet artists sharing the same vision of music, and experiment with new things, even when the production budget was limited."

CARTER KAYA

Discover the French musical empire Delit Music France and its visionary leader Carter Kaya.

Paris, February 11, 2023 – Delit Music France, the French subsidiary of major Delit Music and Delit Music Group, is proud to introduce its director, Bertrand Carter Kaya. This talented hip-hop artist, composer, sound engineer, screenwriter, director, photographer, webmaster and graphic designer founded Delit Entertainement and Delit Music Group in 2012 in the 11th arrondissement of Paris and today located in 94500, Champigny sur Marne.

Delit Music France is a leading company in the French music and audiovisual industry. It is comprised of several active subsidiaries such as Actu Music France, Info Music, Delit Face, Music Subscription, and the DMG Records association. DMG Records is the first music production structure created by Carter Kaya in 2005 in the 17th arrondissement of Paris and is composed of a 2k Studio recording studio.

Delit Music France is proud to produce talented artists such as:

Leena Blige,
Tracy, B-la, Nya, B.Carter, Alisson, Lise, Tyron, Doly, Mona Lisa, Sista, Makenzi, Les Récidivistes, Lil Son, Makenzi, and Les Récidivistes. Delit Music Group and DMG Records have also collaborated with many international artists such as Aneessa, Dorsey Sick Joker, CNM, Sinik, Joce, Abad Boomsong,
Tracy Kendricks, Locky Style, Ami Eliano, Mr Folly, Maître Tigre, Ellena Jenny, DCL, Express Omégaz, Aconit, Oz, Rachel Even, Krimemind, Yasmina Ousman, Jennifer, Milita, Maryna Lovely, Mélisande Croset, Gaïle, Groupe Bana Laumière, Vision Bass, Mushapata, Matatastar, Mandombe Ba Ntou.

Delit Music Group has also collaborated with:

companies such as Iggy Magazine, IndieZone Mag, Pump It Up Magazine (Los Angeles), Dorss Prod, Gashy Production, Africa Dance Company, K-Prod, City Zik Performance Hall, Le Grand Jeu Zaba Kuzinga (Association), KMF TV, Écho Mondiale France, Angola Independence Day 2013 (City Zik) & Angola Independence Day 2017 (Antonio Lukeba).
Finally, Delit Music Records collaborated with singer Mona Lisa for her single entitled "I Love Paris" by producing the instrumental and mixing.

JOIN THE PARTY WITH B. CARTER MAN'S "FIESTA"

B. Carter Kaya Man's latest single "Fiesta" is not just any hip-hop track. It's a song that is designed to make you move and have fun. As soon as the beat starts, you'll find it hard to resist the urge to get up and dance. The catchy lyrics encourage you to move your hips and follow the rhythm, inviting you to join the party.

One of the unique features of "Fiesta" is B. Carter Man's voice. He uses his distinct vocal style to breathe life into the lyrics, conveying a sense of fun, energy, and enthusiasm that is contagious.

With every word, he encourages his fans to let loose and let their bodies move to the music.

The lyrics of "Fiesta" are an invitation to come together and celebrate life. They encourage listeners to forget their worries and immerse themselves in the moment, fully enjoying every second of the party.

Whether you're a hip-hop fan or simply in the mood for some upbeat and joyful music, "Fiesta" by B. Carter Man is the perfect track to get you in the groove.

So, what are you waiting for? Pre-order "Fiesta" now and be one of the first to experience this high-energy and fun-filled track. "Fiesta" will be available on March 24th, so mark your calendars and get ready to dance the night away!

WAS THE GREEN BOOK A GUIDE TO FREEDOM OR A CONSTRAINT ON BLACK TRAVEL?

The Green Book, also known as the Negro Motorist Green Book, was a travel guide published from 1936 to 1966 that aimed to help African American travelers navigate a country where they faced widespread racial discrimination. The guide listed hotels, restaurants, gas stations, and other establishments that were safe and welcoming to black travelers during a time when many businesses would refuse to serve them.

There are several different podcast platforms that each reach millions of users on a daily basis. For instance, Apple's iTunes service has a podcast feature that is utilized by millions of listeners around the world every single day. This means that if you invest the time and energy into sharing a top-quality podcast to that network, you will have the chance of reaching an enormous audience by using a relatively simple and accessible method.

However, while the Green Book was intended to help African Americans travel with greater ease and safety, it also had a more complex legacy. Some argue that the guide perpetuated the idea of segregation and limited the freedom of black travelers by dictating where they could and could not go. In this way, the Green Book was not just a guide to freedom, but also a constraint on black travel.

One of the major challenges faced by African American travelers during this time was the lack of safe places to stay and eat. Many hotels and restaurants refused to serve black customers, and the few that did were often substandard. The Green Book sought to address this issue by providing a comprehensive list of establishments that were willing to welcome black travelers. This helped to ensure that African Americans could travel with a degree of safety and comfort that was previously unavailable to them.

However, while the Green Book did provide a measure of protection to black travelers, it also reinforced the idea of segregation and limited their freedom to travel as they pleased. The guide only listed establishments that were safe for black travelers, but it did not challenge the systemic racial discrimination that made such a guide necessary in the first place.

Furthermore, by dictating where black travelers could go, the Green Book limited their freedom to explore and experience new places. The guide restricted black travelers to a specific set of establishments, rather than allowing them to venture off the beaten path and discover new places on their own. In this way, the Green Book perpetuated the idea of segregation and limited the freedom of black travelers.

In conclusion, while the Green Book was intended to help African American travelers navigate a country where they faced widespread racial discrimination, it also had a more complex legacy. While the guide provided a measure of safety and comfort to black travelers, it also perpetuated the idea of segregation and limited their freedom to travel as they pleased. The Green Book was a guide to freedom for some, but for others, it was a constraint on black travel.
Many famous musicians used the Green Book during their travels. Some of these include:
Louis Armstrong
Duke Ellington
Nat King Cole
Ella Fitzgerald
Sarah Vaughan
The Green Book to help them navigate a country where racial discrimination made traveling as an African American a challenging and often dangerous experience. Despite the limitations imposed by the guide, it provided a measure of safety and comfort for these musicians as they traveled and performed across the country.

THE EVOLUTION OF SOUL FOOD:
A JOURNEY THROUGH BLACK CULINARY HISTORY & RECIPES

Soul food is a culinary tradition that has its roots in the cuisine of African American slaves. Born out of necessity and limited resources, soul food is a testament to the ingenuity and resilience of black people in America. Over the years, soul food has undergone a significant evolution, and today it remains an integral part of black culture and a celebration of black culinary heritage.

Soul food has its roots in the cuisine of African slaves who were brought to America in the 16th and 17th centuries. Forced to work long hours on plantations, slaves had to make do with the ingredients that were readily available to them. They made use of the animals and crops that were deemed unfit for their owners, such as pigs' feet, ham hocks, and collard greens. The dishes that were created from these ingredients became known as soul food and were a reflection of the ingenuity and resourcefulness of black people.

Over the years, soul food has undergone a significant evolution. As black people migrated from the South to the North and West, they brought their culinary traditions with them. They adapted their recipes to the ingredients that were available in their new communities, resulting in regional variations of soul food, such as Texan barbecue, Southern fried chicken, and Midwestern cornbread.

Despite the evolution of soul food, certain dishes remain staples of the cuisine. Fried chicken, collard greens, and cornbread are just a few of the dishes that have become synonymous with soul food. These dishes are not only delicious but also steeped in cultural and historical significance. They represent a connection to the past and a celebration of black culinary heritage.

Today, soul food continues to play an important role in black culture. Whether it is enjoyed at a family gathering or in a restaurant, soul food remains a symbol of black resilience and creativity. It is a cuisine that has been passed down from generation to generation and continues to evolve with the times.

In conclusion, soul food is a culinary tradition that has undergone a significant evolution over the years. From its roots in the cuisine of African American slaves to its present-day iteration, soul food remains an integral part of black culture and a celebration of black culinary heritage. Whether you are a seasoned cook or just starting out, exploring the evolution of soul food is a journey through black culinary history that is well worth taking.

Fried Chicken:

Ingredients:
4 lbs chicken pieces (thighs, legs, breasts)
2 cups buttermilk
2 tsp hot sauce
2 cups all-purpose flour
2 tsp paprika
2 tsp garlic powder
2 tsp salt
1 tsp black pepper
Oil for frying

Instructions:

In a large bowl, combine the buttermilk and hot sauce. Add the chicken pieces and let marinate for at least 30 minutes or up to overnight.
In another large bowl, combine the flour, paprika, garlic powder, salt, and pepper.
Remove the chicken from the buttermilk mixture, allowing any excess to drip off.
Dredge each piece of chicken in the flour mixture, making sure to coat well.
In a large, deep skillet or Dutch oven, heat about 1 inch of oil to 350°F.
Fry the chicken in batches, turning occasionally, until the coating is crispy and golden brown and the chicken is cooked through, about 15 minutes.
Drain on paper towels and serve hot.

BLACK HISTORY MONTH

COLLARD GREENS RECIPE

1. 1 lb collard greens, washed, stemmed, and chopped
2. 1 large smoked ham hock
3. 1 medium yellow onion, diced
4. 2 cloves garlic, minced
5. 4 cups chicken broth
6. 1 tbsp apple cider vinegar
7. 1 tbsp brown sugar
8. 1 tsp salt
9. 1/2 tsp black pepper

1. Rinse the collard greens and chop them into small pieces.
2. In a large pot, place the ham hock and enough water to cover. Bring to a boil, then reduce heat to low and simmer for 1 hour.
3. Remove the ham hock from the pot and let it cool. Reserve the broth.
4. When the ham hock is cool enough to handle, remove the meat from the bone and chop it into small pieces.
5. In the same pot, add the onion, garlic, and a little bit of oil. Cook over medium heat until the onion is softened.
6. Stir in the collard greens and cook until they are wilted, about 5-7 minutes.
7. Pour in the chicken broth and 2 cups of the reserved ham broth. Add the apple cider vinegar, brown sugar, salt, and black pepper.
8. Stir in the chopped ham and bring the mixture to a boil.
9. Reduce heat to low, cover, and simmer for 1-2 hours, or until the collard greens are tender and the flavors have developed.
10. Serve hot with cornbread, if desired.

For more recipes, visit us at www.pumpitupmagazine.com

MAC & CHEESE RECIPE

Ingredients:

8 oz elbow macaroni

4 tbsp unsalted butter

4 tbsp all-purpose flour

3 cups whole milk

1 tsp salt

1/2 tsp black pepper

1/4 tsp nutmeg

8 oz grated cheddar cheese

4 oz grated parmesan cheese

Cook the macaroni according to package instructions until al dente. Drain and set aside.

In a large saucepan, melt the butter over medium heat.

Stir in the flour and cook for 2-3 minutes, until the mixture is smooth and bubbly.

Gradually add the milk, whisking continuously to prevent lumps from forming.

Cook the sauce, stirring frequently, until it thickens, about 5-7 minutes.

Stir in the salt, pepper, nutmeg, and grated cheddar cheese. Cook until the cheese is melted and the sauce is smooth.

Stir in the cooked macaroni until well combined.

Transfer the mixture to a 9x13 inch baking dish and sprinkle with grated parmesan cheese.

Bake at 375°F for 20-25 minutes, or until the top is golden brown and the cheese is melted.

Serve hot and enjoy!

For more recipes, visit us at www.pumpitupmagazine.com

AN AMERICAN GAL'S COOKBOOK: DISCOVERING DELICIOUS RECIPES AND FASCINATING HISTORIES ACROSS THE 50 STATES BY BOBBI JO LATHAN

COOK NOW

Funk Therapy

| Funky | Trendy | Cool | Hip |

Wear The Music You Love!

Visit our merchandise store on our website:

WWW.FUNKTHERAPYMUSIC.COM

10% Discount code: STAYFUNKY

- Hoodies
- Crop Top
- Sweat Pants
- Bucket Hats
- Slides
- Mugs

UNISEX T-SHIRTS

Brown T-Shirt

GRAB IT NOW

Orange T-Shirt

GRAB IT NOW

Beige T-Shirts

GRAB IT NOW

Join our community
@funktherapy2

CELEBRATING THE CONTRIBUTIONS OF BLACK ARTISTS, WRITERS, AND PERFORMERS

Throughout history, Black artists, writers, and performers have made invaluable contributions to the world of art, literature, and entertainment. Despite facing numerous obstacles and barriers, they have consistently pushed the boundaries of what is possible, producing work that is innovative, powerful, and timeless. Today, it is important to celebrate the legacy of these talented individuals, to acknowledge their contributions to the world of art and culture, and to inspire future generations to continue their legacy.

One of the most significant contributions made by Black artists is their influence on the visual arts. From the Harlem Renaissance of the 1920s to the Civil Rights movement of the 1960s and beyond, Black artists have been at the forefront of artistic movements and styles, producing works that explore the complexities of race, identity, and social justice. From the bold and colorful paintings of Jacob Lawrence to the powerful and thought-provoking sculptures of Augusta Savage, Black artists have inspired countless others with their unique perspectives and fearless approach to their work.

Black writers have also made an indelible mark on the literary world, exploring a wide range of themes and styles, from historical fiction to science fiction and beyond. From the powerful works of Toni Morrison to the groundbreaking poems of Maya Angelou, Black writers have challenged societal norms and paved the way for new voices and perspectives to be heard. Through their words, they have given voice to the experiences of Black people, illuminating the triumphs and struggles of their communities, and inspiring others to fight for justice and equality.

In the world of performance, Black artists have also made an immense impact, from the early days of vaudeville and jazz, to the vibrant music scenes of today. From the soulful melodies of Ray Charles to the powerful performances of Beyoncé, Black performers have entertained and inspired audiences with their incredible talent and creative energy. Whether they are dancing, singing, or acting, they have consistently brought new perspectives and ideas to the stage, capturing the hearts and minds of audiences around the world.

In conclusion, the contributions made by Black artists, writers, and performers cannot be overstated. Through their works, they have challenged us to see the world in new and exciting ways, to think about the issues that matter most, and to imagine a world where everyone is equal and free. As we continue to celebrate their legacy, we must also work to ensure that future generations have the opportunity to continue this great tradition, to produce works that are innovative, powerful, and timeless. By doing so, we can help ensure that their contributions will live on for many years to come.

Emmerson

SIERRA LEONE SINGER EMMERSON IS SETTING THE TONE WITH A NEW INFECTIOUS BANGER

"GI ME THAT"

⚪ 📷 @EMMBOCKMUSIC  EMMBOCKMUSIC

WWW.EMMBOCK.COM

ANEESSA
MICHAEL B. SUTTON

I FOUND MYSELF IN YOU

OUT NOW

WWW.THESOUNDOFLA.COM

*Smooth Jazz Love Song
for An Essential Romantic Playlist
Capturing the joyful essence of
what it feels like
to love and be loved!*

Editions L.A.

DIGITAL CREATIVE AGENCY

We Transform Your Vision Into Creative Results

Editions L.A. is a full-service agency based in Los Angeles. Our company is a collective of amazing people striving to build delightful services
We believe that is all about getting your message across clearly and with a "Wow!" thrown in for good measure.

Our Awesome Services

Branding

We build, style and tone your brand identity from the ground up.
We rebrand established bands, brands or businesses.

Merchandise Store
Website design and E-Commerce
Website updates

Digital Marketing

CD Cover | Banners | Logo design | Flyers | Brochures |
Leaflets | Print ads | Magazine covers & artworks
Facebook / twitter / instagram / youtube artworks
| Book cover
Infographics | Icon Design |
| TshirtsProduct Labels | Presentation slides
Corporate graphics
Professional photo editing & enhancing
Redesign existing elements
YouTube Optimization and Monetization
Youtube Video Editing
Lyric Video and Advertising Design.

Publishing

BOOK COVER DESIGN
EBOOK FORMATTING SERVICES
and distribution on major platforms
(Amazon, Barnes & Nobles..)

Tell us about your dream and we will make it true!

Editions L.A.
7210 Jordan Avenue Suite B42, Canoga Park, California 91303, United States
info@edtions-la.com
Website: www.editions-la.com

BEING SINGLE ON VALENTINE'S DAY: THE JOURNEY OF SELF-DISCOVERY AND KNOW THYSELF

Valentine's Day is often associated with romantic love, couples, and all things heart-shaped. However, for those who are single, this day can often be a source of stress, anxiety, and feelings of loneliness or unworthiness. But instead of focusing on what one may lack, it's an opportunity to focus on oneself and embark on a journey of self-discovery and growth.

One of the key benefits of being single is the ability to focus on one's own needs, wants, and desires. Without the pressure of meeting someone else's expectations, one can spend time and energy exploring their passions, interests, and hobbies. This can lead to a deeper sense of self-awareness and a better understanding of what truly brings one happiness and fulfillment.

Being single also provides the opportunity to practice self-care. This can range from activities such as exercising regularly, eating nutritious food, and engaging in mindfulness and meditation practices. Focusing on physical and mental wellness can lead to increased levels of confidence, self-esteem, and overall happiness.

In addition, being single allows for the time and space to cultivate meaningful relationships with friends and family. Whether it's spending time with close friends, volunteering in one's community, or connecting with family members, relationships with those who truly care and support one can bring immense joy and satisfaction.

Moreover, being single provides the chance to focus on personal growth and development. Whether it's taking classes, reading books, or learning a new skill, investing time and energy in oneself can bring a sense of accomplishment and fulfillment. This can also lead to increased self-confidence and the ability to tackle new challenges with a positive attitude.

In conclusion, being single on Valentine's Day can be a journey of self-discovery and growth. Instead of focusing on what one may lack, it's an opportunity to focus on oneself, engage in self-care practices, build meaningful relationships, and invest time in personal growth and development. By embracing one's individuality and focusing on what brings them happiness and fulfillment, one can live a fulfilling and rewarding life.

ARE YOU TIRED OF BEING SINGLE? HOW & WHERE TO FIND YOUR SOULMATE

Finding your soulmate can be a lifelong journey filled with ups and downs, twists and turns, but ultimately, a journey worth taking. Your soulmate is someone who will understand and love you for who you are, someone who will be your partner in life, and your rock through the good times and the bad. But where do you start your search for this special person? How do you find the one who will share your life and your heart? Here are some tips on how and where to find your soulmate.

Work on yourself first: Before you can attract someone special into your life, you need to love and accept yourself for who you are. Focus on your personal growth, pursue your passions, and be comfortable in your own skin. The more you love yourself, the easier it will be to attract someone who loves you too.

Be open-minded: Your soulmate may come from an unexpected place, so be open to new experiences and keep an open mind. Join new clubs, attend social events, and explore new hobbies and interests. The more you put yourself out there, the more opportunities you'll have to meet new people.

Get involved in the community: Volunteering, joining local clubs and organizations, or participating in community events can be a great way to meet new people, make new friends, and potentially find your soulmate. By giving back to your community, you can also demonstrate your values, interests, and passions, attracting someone who shares your ideals.

Online dating: In today's digital age, online dating can be a convenient and effective way to meet new people and find your soulmate. Choose a reputable dating site and create a thoughtful profile that reflects who you are. Be honest about what you're looking for and take the time to get to know others before meeting in person.

Ask for help: Don't be afraid to ask your friends and family to introduce you to someone new. They may know someone who would be a great match for you. Additionally, consider hiring a professional matchmaker or coach who can help guide you through the process and provide you with additional resources and support.

In conclusion, finding your soulmate can be a journey that takes time and effort, but it can also be one of the most rewarding experiences of your life. Remember, the journey is as important as the destination, so be patient, trust the process, and enjoy the ride.

COUPLE'S WORKOUTS:
A BONDING EXPERIENCE FOR FITNESS AND RELATIONSHIPS

Working out together can be a fun and effective way to bond with your significant other while also improving your physical health. Not only will you be able to support and motivate each other, but you'll also have the opportunity to create new memories and strengthen your relationship. Here are some ideas for couple's workouts that you can try together:

Outdoor activities: Going for a walk, hike, or bike ride together can be a great way to enjoy the beautiful outdoors while getting some exercise. Try to find a new trail or park to explore each week to keep things fresh and exciting.

Group fitness classes: Trying a new workout together, such as yoga, Pilates, or dance, can be a fun and unique bonding experience. Not only will you be able to challenge each other physically, but you'll also have the opportunity to learn and grow together.

Home workouts: If you're short on time or don't want to go to the gym, consider doing a workout together at home. There are many online resources available with at-home workouts that can be done with minimal equipment.

Competitive games: Incorporating some friendly competition into your workout can make it even more enjoyable. Try playing a game of basketball, tennis, or even a friendly race to add an extra challenge and some fun.

Weight lifting: If you're both looking to build strength, consider lifting weights together. Not only will you be able to spot each other and keep each other safe, but you'll also have the opportunity to push each other to new limits.

In conclusion, incorporating physical activity into your relationship can be a great way to bond with your significant other while also improving your health. So, whether you're trying a new fitness class, exploring the outdoors, or lifting weights together, make sure to have fun and enjoy each other's company. Remember, the journey is as important as the destination, so be patient, trust the process, and enjoy the ride.

4 WEEKS FULL BODY WORKOUT CHALLENGE

Week 1 — Focus on your form

Sunday	Lower Body
Monday	Upper Body
Tuesday	Cross Training
Wednesday	Total Body
Thursday	Abs
Friday	Cross Training
Saturday	Rest Time

Week 2 — Go for more reps

Sunday	Lower Body
Monday	Upper Body
Tuesday	Cross Training
Wednesday	Total Body
Thursday	Abs
Friday	Cross Training
Saturday	Rest Time

Week 3 — Try a new cross-training workout

Sunday	Lower Body
Monday	Upper Body
Tuesday	Cross Training
Wednesday	Total Body
Thursday	Abs
Friday	Cross Training
Saturday	Rest Time

Week 4 — Complete and Extra Round

Sunday	Lower Body
Monday	Upper Body
Tuesday	Cross Training
Wednesday	Total Body
Thursday	Abs
Friday	Cross Training
Saturday	Rest Time

Pump it up

FROM WALKING TO RUNNING
4 Weeks Fit Challenge

	1st Week	2nd Week	3rd Week	4th Week
SUN	5 Mins Steady Run 1 Mins Walk Repat 3x	5 Mins Steady Run 1 Mins Walk Repat 4x	5 Mins Steady Run 2 Mins Walk Repat 5x	5 Mins Steady Run 2 Mins Walk Repat 6x
MON	7 Mins Steady Run 1 Mins Walk Repat 3x	8 Mins Steady Run 2 Mins Walk Repat 4x	10 Mins Steady Run 3 Mins Walk Repat 5x	12 Mins Steady Run 3 Mins Walk Repat 6x
TUE	REST DAY	REST DAY	REST DAY	REST DAY
WED	7 Mins Steady Run 1 Mins Walk Repat 3x	Speed Intervals	20 Mins Progression Run	Body Weight Strength Workout
THU	15 Mins Easy Run or Walk	15 Progression Run	Speed Intervals	Speed Intervals
FRI	REST DAY	REST DAY	REST DAY	REST DAY
SAT	Speed Intervals	Body Weight Strength Workout	Body Weight Strength Workout	30 Mins Progression Run

YOUR MUSIC CONSULTANT

"YOU BELIEVE, SO DO WE!"

We Can Help You To Grow Your Business

We are a monthly based service, we put faith in artists who has major potential, believed in them, and who are willing to spend their time and own money to work with us in building a successful music career!

Digital Marketing Services

SOCIAL MEDIA - STREAMING SERVICES - MUSIC DISTRIBUTION - PRESS RELEASE - PRESS DISTRIBUTION - PR

Radio Airplay and TV Commercial

TERRESTRIAL AND DIGITAL RADIO CAMPAIGN AL GENRES EXCEPT HEAVY METAL - CABLE TV AND MAJOR NETWORK COMMERCIAL

Licensing & Booking

CONCERTS, LIVE MUSIC, EVENTS, CLUB NIGHTS - RED CARPETS - FOREIGN LICENSING AND SUBOPUBLISHING

Why Choose Us ?

3 DECADES OF MUSIC BUSINESS EXPERIENCE
Platinum and Gold Records
MOTOWN RECORDS
UNIVERSAL
SONY
CAPITOL RECORDS

WE WORKED WITH:
Kanye West - Jay Z - Stevie Wonder - Michael Jackson - Germaine Jackson - Smokey Robinson - Dionne Warwick - Cheryl Lynn - The Originals -

📞 **1-818-514-0038**
(Ext. 1)
Monday - Friday / 9am to 6pm

FIND US :

www.YourMusicConsultant.com
30721 Russell Ranch Road Suite 140 Westlake Village, USA
Email : info@yourmusicconsultant.com

TOP TIPS

INDIE ARTIST: HOW TO BOOK YOUR NEXT GIG

As an indie artist, booking gigs can be a challenging and competitive process. However, with the rig strategy and preparation, you can increase your chances of landing the gigs you want and build yo reputation as a professional artist. Here are some tips for booking your next gig:

Build a strong online presence: A strong online presence is essential for indie artists looking to bo gigs. Make sure to have a professional website or social media page where potential clients can lea about your work, see your portfolio, and contact you for booking inquiries.

Network: Networking is key in the music industry, and it's important to make connections with oth musicians, venue owners, and booking agents. Attend local music events, join online music commu ties, and reach out to other musicians and industry professionals to build your network.

Offer a professional and polished package: When reaching out to potential clients, make sure to of a professional and polished package that includes a well-crafted press kit, high-quality audio recor ings, and professional photos. This will increase your chances of standing out from the competition a making a lasting impression.

Be proactive: Don't wait for gigs to come to you - actively seek out opportunities to perform. Look f open mic nights, local events, and other opportunities to showcase your talent. Be prepared to perfor at a moment's notice and take advantage of every opportunity to perform in front of a live audience

Be flexible: Be open to performing in different venues and at different events, and be willing to adju your performance style to fit the venue or event. This will increase your chances of booking gigs and e panding your audience.

Price yourself fairly: Make sure to price yourself fairly and negotiate a fair fee for your performances Be prepared to discuss your fees, negotiate, and make compromises if necessary, but don't underval your talent and experience.

Follow up: After reaching out to potential clients, make sure to follow up with a friendly and professio al email or call. This will show that you are interested in the gig and will increase your chances of landi the booking.

In conclusion, booking gigs as an indie artist requires effort, persistence, and a strong online presen By networking, offering a professional package, being proactive, and pricing yourself fairly, you can crease your chances of landing the gigs you want and building your reputation as a professional arti So, go out there, be confident, and let your talent shine!

VALENTINE'S DAY MOVIE PICKS: CLASSIC LOVE STORIES

Valentine's Day is a time to celebrate love and affection, and what better way to do so than by watching a classic love story on the big screen? Whether you're in a relationship or single, these timeless movies are sure to bring a smile to your face and a warm feeling to your heart. Here are some classic love stories that are perfect for a Valentine's Day movie night:

"Casablanca" (1942): Set in Morocco during World War II, "Casablanca" is a classic love story that tells the tale of a man torn between love and duty. Starring Humphrey Bogart and Ingrid Bergman, the movie is a timeless tale of love and sacrifice that is sure to capture your heart.

"Roman Holiday" (1953): Starring Gregory Peck and Audrey Hepburn, "Roman Holiday" is a classic love story set in Rome. This movie follows the adventures of a princess on a tour of Europe who falls in love with a reporter, leading to a charming and unforgettable romance.

"The Notebook" (2004): Based on the novel by Nicholas Sparks, "The Notebook" is a timeless love story that spans several decades. Starring Ryan Gosling and Rachel McAdams, this movie tells the tale of a couple's love that endures the test of time.

"When Harry Met Sally" (1989): This classic romantic comedy is a timeless love story that explores the age-old question of whether men and women can ever truly be just friends. Starring Billy Crystal and Meg Ryan, this movie is sure to make you laugh and cry.

"Sleepless in Seattle" (1993): Starring Tom Hanks and Meg Ryan, "Sleepless in Seattle" is a classic love story about a man and a woman who fall in love over the radio. This movie is a heartwarming tale of love and destiny that is sure to touch your heart.

"Titanic" (1997): Starring Kate Winslet and Leonardo DiCaprio, "Titanic" is a classic love story that follows the tragic romance between a wealthy woman and a poor artist aboard the ill-fated ocean liner. This movie is a timeless tale of love and loss that is sure to captivate you.

In conclusion, these classic love stories are the perfect way to celebrate Valentine's Day with your significant other or with a group of friends. So, pop some popcorn, grab a box of tissues, and settle in for a night of romance and nostalgia. Happy Valentine's Day!

REBUILDING HOPE: SUPPORTING THE VICTIMS OF THE SYRIA-TURKEY EARTHQUAKE

A devastating earthquake struck the border region between Turkey and Syria, killing over 20,000 people and injuring thousands more. The magnitude 6.8 earthquake was felt as in Syria, and Turkey. The earthquake caused widespread damage to buildings, infrastructure, and homes, leaving many people homeless and in need of immediate assistance.

In times of crisis, it is important to come together and support those in need. The victims of the Syria-Turkey earthquake need our help to rebuild their homes and their lives. Here are some ways to support the victims and contribute to the rebuilding efforts:

Donate to humanitarian organizations: There are many international humanitarian organizations, such as the International Red Cross and UNICEF, working to provide immediate assistance to the victims of the earthquake. These organizations are providing food, water, shelter, and medical care to those in need. You can donate money to these organizations to help support their efforts.

Volunteer: If you have the skills and expertise needed to help with the rebuilding efforts, consider volunteering your time and resources. Organizations such as Habitat for Humanity and Engineers Without Borders are working to rebuild homes and infrastructure in the affected areas.

Raise Awareness: Share information about the earthquake and the needs of the victims with your friends, family, and social media networks. Raising awareness about the situation can help bring more attention and support to the cause.

Support local businesses: Supporting local businesses in the affected areas can help provide a much-needed economic boost to the communities affected by the earthquake. Purchase goods and services from local merchants to help support their recovery.

In conclusion, the earthquake in Turkey and Syria has had a devastating impact on the people and communities affected. However, by coming together and supporting the victims, we can help rebuild hope and create a brighter future for those affected.

Every little bit helps, so consider how you can contribute and make a difference today.

LET'S HELP SYRIA & TURKEY!

WITH DONATION TO HELP REFUGEES WHO WERE IMPACTED BY THE EARTHQUAKE

DONATE NOW

Your donation will help us provide emergency services to families in Turkey and Syria and refugee families in countries around the world. Please give what you can today.

HTTPS://HELP.RESCUE.ORG/

www.ingramcontent.com/pod-product-compliance
Lightning Source LLC
Chambersburg PA
CBHW080901010526
44118CB00015B/2231